To every parent and guardian – Your care and wisdom light the way for the next generation. This book is a small tribute to your endless efforts in keeping children safe and empowered.

Table of Content

Introduction

The Digital Age: A New Parenting Challenge

Parenting has always been a complex and rewarding journey, but in today's digital age, the challenges are more unique and ever-evolving. Unlike past generations, where children's primary interactions happened in schools, playgrounds, and homes, today's kids are growing up in a world where digital devices, social media, and online gaming are an integral part of their daily lives. While technology offers incredible benefits—such as instant communication, limitless learning resources, and global connectivity—it also introduces risks that previous generations of parents never had to consider.

As a parent, you may feel overwhelmed by the fast-changing nature of technology. New apps, social media trends, and online threats emerge almost daily, making it difficult to keep up. How do you ensure your child is safe online? How do you set limits without completely restricting their digital experiences? How do you guide them in using technology responsibly? These are questions many parents struggle with, and this book is designed to provide clear, step-by-step answers.

The key to successful digital parenting is not about banning technology but about creating a safe, structured, and balanced digital environment for your child. With the right knowledge and tools, you can empower your child to make smart and responsible choices while still enjoying the benefits of the digital world.

Why Digital Parenting Matters

Many parents assume that as long as their child is at home, they are safe. However, the internet has changed the way we define safety. The dangers children face today are not just physical but also digital. Cyberbullying, online predators, identity theft, and exposure to inappropriate content are just some of the risks that come with internet access.

Unlike the real world, where you can teach your child to look both ways before crossing the street, the online world has invisible threats. Your child might unknowingly share personal information, interact with strangers, or fall victim to harmful online trends. Digital parenting is essential because it helps bridge the gap between technology and safety.

Additionally, the way children interact with technology can impact their mental and emotional well-being. Excessive screen time, social media pressure, and online validation can contribute to anxiety, stress, and self-esteem issues. By actively guiding your child, you can ensure they develop healthy digital habits that promote emotional balance, critical thinking, and responsible behavior.

Digital parenting is not about controlling every aspect of your child's online life. Instead, it is about teaching them the skills to navigate the digital world safely and independently. When children understand online risks and the importance of digital responsibility, they are more likely to make wise choices even when parents are not watching.

Understanding the Online World Your Child Navigates

The internet is vast, and children interact with it in different ways based on their age, interests, and social environment. Understanding what your child does online is the first step in guiding them toward safe digital habits. Here are some common ways children and teenagers engage with technology:

- **Social Media:** Platforms like TikTok, Instagram, Snapchat, and Discord allow children to connect with friends, share content, and explore trends. However, these platforms also expose them to privacy concerns, cyberbullying, and unrealistic social comparisons.

- **Online Gaming:** Many kids spend hours on multiplayer online games like Minecraft, Roblox, or Fortnite. While these games can be fun and educational, they also come with risks like in-game purchases, cyberbullying, and interaction with strangers.
- **Streaming and Content Consumption:** YouTube, Netflix, and other streaming services provide entertainment and educational content. However, without supervision, children may be exposed to inappropriate videos or misleading information.
- **Messaging Apps and Online Communication:** Messaging apps like WhatsApp, Messenger, and even in-game chats allow kids to communicate with friends. Unfortunately, they also open doors to online predators, scammers, and harmful conversations.
- **Educational and Creative Platforms:** Websites like Khan Academy, Google Classroom, and various creative apps help children learn and explore their talents. Encouraging the use of these platforms can balance entertainment and education in a child's digital life.

Knowing where your child spends time online helps you set appropriate boundaries, implement parental controls, and have open conversations about internet safety.

Common Cyber Threats and Risks

The digital world comes with both opportunities and dangers. Being aware of common cyber threats will help you educate your child about online safety and prepare them to handle challenges. Here are some of the most significant online risks:

1. Cyberbullying

Cyberbullying happens when children are harassed, humiliated, or threatened online through social media, gaming platforms, or messaging apps. Unlike traditional bullying, cyberbullying follows children everywhere, making it harder to escape. Teaching kids how to identify, report, and respond to cyberbullying is crucial.

2. Online Predators

Some individuals use the internet to manipulate and exploit children. Online predators often pretend to be someone they are not to gain a child's trust. They may communicate through social media, games, or private messaging apps. Teaching kids about "stranger danger" online is just as important as teaching them about it in the real world.

3. Privacy and Data Security Risks

Children often share personal information online without realizing its consequences. Posting photos, sharing locations, and filling out online forms can expose them to identity theft, scams, and data breaches. Teaching kids to protect their personal information helps prevent privacy violations.

4. Inappropriate Content

The internet contains content that is not suitable for children, including violence, hate speech, and explicit material. Even with parental controls, children may accidentally come across disturbing images or videos. Teaching kids what to do when they encounter such content is essential for their well-being.

5. Scams and Phishing Attacks

Children can be tricked into clicking on fake links, downloading harmful files, or giving out sensitive information. Scammers often target kids through email, social media, and gaming platforms. Educating children on how to recognize and avoid scams protects them from digital fraud.

Understanding these risks allows you to create a safer digital environment for your child while teaching them to recognize and respond to online dangers responsibly.

How to Use This Book: A Step-by-Step Guide

This book is designed to be a **practical and easy-to-follow guide** for parents who want to safeguard their children in the online world. Here's how you can make the most of it:

- **Start with Understanding**: The first few chapters introduce the digital world, how children interact with technology, and the risks involved. This foundation will help you grasp the importance of digital parenting.
- **Follow the Step-by-Step Strategies**: Each section provides actionable steps for setting up parental controls, monitoring online activities, and teaching kids about online safety.
- **Use the Checklists and Guidelines**: Throughout the book, you'll find helpful checklists and safety guidelines. These will make it easier for you to implement safety measures in your household.
- **Have Conversations with Your Child**: Digital parenting is not just about technology—it's also about communication. The book provides conversation starters and tips on how to talk to your child about online safety without fear or negativity.
- **Apply the Knowledge as You Go**: Instead of reading everything at once, apply the knowledge step by step. Start with basic safety measures and gradually introduce more advanced digital parenting strategies.

By following this book's guidance, you will feel more confident in **protecting your child online** while **empowering them to use technology responsibly**.

Part 1: Understanding the Online World

Chapter 1: The Digital Landscape for Kids

The Rise of the Internet and Social Media

The internet has become a fundamental part of daily life. What started as a tool for communication and research has transformed into a vast digital world where people connect, learn, and entertain themselves. For children and teens, the internet is an extension of their social lives, schoolwork, and entertainment. Unlike past generations who relied on books, television, and outdoor play for learning and fun, today's children interact with the world through digital screens.

Social media has also revolutionized the way kids and teens communicate. Platforms like Facebook, Instagram, Snapchat, TikTok, and YouTube provide a space to share thoughts, experiences, and creativity. Messaging apps, online games, and video streaming services allow them to engage with others across the globe. This rapid digital shift presents both opportunities and challenges for parents, making it essential to understand the role of the internet in their child's life.

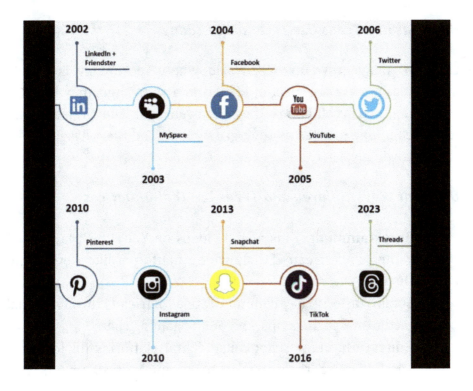

How Social Media Became a Major Part of Childhood

Social media was originally designed for adults to connect, but over time, younger users have joined these platforms. With easy access to smartphones, tablets, and computers, children are now exposed to social media at an early age. Many platforms have minimum age requirements, but children often bypass these by entering false birth dates.

Social media is appealing because it provides instant gratification. A like, comment, or share can boost a child's confidence and make them feel connected. However, it can also lead to an unhealthy dependence on digital validation. Understanding how and why kids engage with social media is the first step in ensuring a balanced and safe digital experience.

How Kids and Teens Use Technology Today

Children today grow up in a world where technology is deeply integrated into every aspect of life. From a young age, they learn to swipe, tap, and scroll before they can even read. Their relationship with technology evolves as they grow older, and their usage habits shift accordingly.

Different Ways Children and Teens Use Digital Devices

- **Entertainment:** Kids watch videos on YouTube, play online games, and stream TV shows on platforms like Netflix and Disney+.
- **Socialization:** They communicate with friends through social media, messaging apps, and online gaming chats.
- **Education:** Many schools use digital platforms for learning, and kids use the internet to complete assignments and projects.
- **Creativity and Expression:** Platforms like TikTok and Instagram allow them to create and share videos, photos, and artwork.
- **Exploration and Curiosity:** Kids search for information, learn new skills, and explore hobbies through online tutorials and articles.

While technology can be a powerful tool for growth, excessive use or exposure to harmful content can have negative consequences. It's essential for parents to guide their children in using digital devices responsibly.

Common Online Platforms and Their Risks (Social Media, Gaming, Messaging Apps)

The digital world is vast, and children interact with various platforms that serve different purposes. Each comes with its own benefits and risks. Parents should be aware of the most popular platforms and how they impact their children.

Social Media Platforms

Social media is where kids connect, share, and express themselves. Popular platforms include:

- **Instagram:** Used for sharing photos and videos. Risk: Exposure to unrealistic beauty standards and cyberbullying.
- **TikTok:** A video-sharing platform known for its short, engaging clips. Risk: Inappropriate content and potential privacy issues.
- **Snapchat:** A messaging app with disappearing messages and filters. Risk: Strangers adding children, sharing of inappropriate content.
- **YouTube:** A platform for watching and creating videos. Risk: Exposure to inappropriate content, even with parental controls.

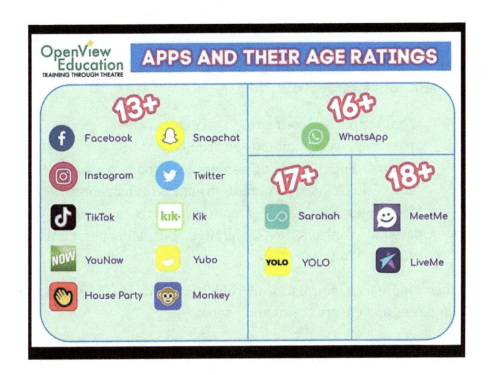

Gaming Platforms

Many kids and teens spend hours on gaming platforms that allow them to interact with others.

- **Roblox:** A virtual gaming world with user-created games. Risk: Online predators, in-game purchases.
- **Fortnite:** A popular battle game with in-game chats. Risk: Exposure to violent content, cyberbullying.
- **Minecraft:** A creative world-building game. Risk: Unregulated chatrooms where strangers can interact with kids.

Messaging Apps

Communication apps are widely used for chatting with friends, but they also pose security risks.

- **WhatsApp:** Used for texting, voice calls, and video calls. Risk: Spam messages, unmonitored group chats.
- **Discord:** Popular among gamers for group chats and voice calls. Risk: Unfiltered content, strangers in chatrooms.
- **Messenger Kids:** A safer option for kids to message with parental controls. Risk: Limited but still potential for cyberbullying.

Understanding these platforms helps parents set appropriate boundaries and ensure their child's safety.

The Psychological Impact of Digital Exposure on Children

Technology offers many benefits, but excessive digital exposure can impact a child's mental and emotional well-being. It's important to recognize the effects and help children develop a healthy relationship with the digital world.

Positive Effects of Technology

- **Educational Opportunities:** Access to online learning resources helps children develop skills and knowledge.
- **Social Connectivity:** Children can stay in touch with family and friends, even from a distance.

- **Creativity and Innovation:** Digital platforms allow kids to create music, videos, and art.
- **Problem-Solving Skills:** Games and online activities can improve cognitive skills and logical thinking.

Negative Effects of Excessive Digital Use

- **Screen Addiction:** Overuse of screens can make kids restless, anxious, and disconnected from real-life activities.
- **Mental Health Issues:** Excessive social media use can lead to anxiety, depression, and self-esteem issues.
- **Sleep Disruptions:** The blue light from screens affects sleep patterns, leading to fatigue and concentration problems.
- **Shortened Attention Span:** Constant scrolling and quick entertainment may reduce a child's ability to focus for long periods.
- **Social Isolation:** Too much online time can take away from real-life friendships and face-to-face interactions.

How Parents Can Help

- **Set Screen Time Limits:** Create a balance between online and offline activities.
- **Encourage Outdoor Play:** Physical activity is crucial for mental and physical well-being.
- **Have Open Conversations:** Talk about the risks and benefits of technology.
- **Lead by Example:** Children imitate their parents, so practice healthy digital habits yourself.
- **Use Parental Controls:** Monitor and guide your child's online activities.

Final Thoughts

The digital landscape for kids is constantly evolving, and as a parent, staying informed is the best way to protect and guide your child. By understanding the platforms they use, the risks involved, and the impact of digital exposure, you can create a safe and positive online experience for them. The key is balance—helping them enjoy the benefits of technology while protecting them from its dangers.

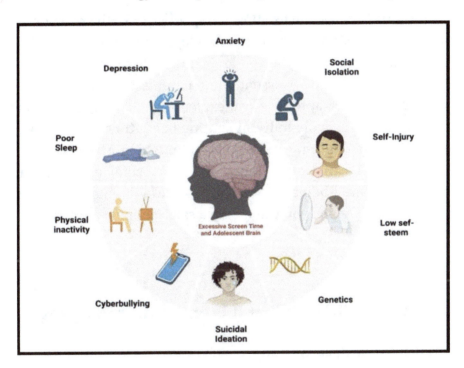

Excessive screen time can be dangerous

Chapter 2: Cyber Threats Every Parent Should Know

The internet is a vast and exciting place, but just like the real world, it has its dangers. As parents, understanding these threats is the first step toward protecting your child. Many of these dangers are not always visible, making it essential for parents to be informed and proactive. In this chapter, we will explore five major online threats that children face: **cyberbullying, online predators, privacy risks, inappropriate content, and scams or phishing attacks.** Each of these risks can significantly impact a child's mental, emotional, and even physical well-being. By recognizing these threats and learning how to address them, you can create a safer online environment for your child.

Cyberbullying: What It Is and How It Happens

Understanding Cyberbullying

Cyberbullying is bullying that takes place over digital platforms such as social media, text messages, online forums, and gaming communities. Unlike traditional bullying, cyberbullying does not end when a child leaves school—it follows them everywhere their device goes. It can involve spreading rumors, sharing embarrassing photos, sending hurtful messages, or even impersonating someone online.

How Cyberbullying Happens

Children can experience cyberbullying in many ways, and it often happens without parents realizing it. Some common forms include:

- **Harassment** – Sending repeated, offensive, or threatening messages.
- **Doxxing** – Sharing private or personal information to embarrass or harm someone.
- **Impersonation** – Creating fake profiles to mock, embarrass, or harm another child.
- **Exclusion** – Leaving someone out of online groups or chats intentionally.

- **Public Humiliation** – Posting personal photos or secrets online without permission.

How Parents Can Help

- **Talk to Your Child** – Make sure they feel comfortable discussing their online experiences with you.
- **Monitor Their Online Activity** – Set boundaries on device usage and check their social media presence.
- **Teach Digital Etiquette** – Encourage your child to treat others with kindness online.
- **Report and Block Bullies** – Show your child how to report harmful content and block offenders.
- **Save Evidence** – If cyberbullying occurs, take screenshots and report them to school officials or authorities if necessary.

Online Predators: How They Target Kids

Who Are Online Predators?

Online predators are adults who use the internet to exploit or manipulate children. They often disguise their true identity and intentions, pretending to be a child's friend to gain their trust. These predators use various tactics to lure children into unsafe situations.

How Predators Target Kids

Online predators use several strategies to befriend and manipulate children, including:

- **Grooming** – Building a friendship over time to gain a child's trust before exploiting them.
- **Flattery and Gifts** – Sending compliments, money, or online game credits to establish trust.
- **Manipulation** – Convincing a child to keep conversations secret from parents.
- **Threats** – If a child refuses to comply, predators may use threats to scare them.
- **Using Fake Profiles** – Pretending to be a peer or celebrity to gain attention.

Protecting Your Child

- **Teach Online Stranger Awareness** – Just as in the real world, children should not talk to strangers online.
- **Set Privacy Settings** – Restrict who can contact your child on social media and messaging apps.
- **Monitor Online Friends** – Regularly review your child's friend lists and online conversations.
- **Encourage Open Communication** – Let your child know they can always come to you if someone online makes them uncomfortable.
- **Use Parental Controls** – Enable safety filters that limit communication with unknown users.

Privacy Risks: The Dangers of Oversharing

Why Privacy Matters Online

Every time your child shares personal information online, they leave a digital footprint. This data can be misused for cyberbullying, identity theft, or even to locate them in real life. Oversharing can happen through social media posts, gaming profiles, or even school forums.

What Information Should Not Be Shared?

- **Full Name and Address** – Reveals personal identity and home location.
- **School Name and Routine** – Can be used by strangers to track them.

- **Phone Number and Email** – Leads to spam, scams, or phishing attacks.
- **Personal Photos and Videos** – Can be misused or manipulated.
- **Passwords and Login Details** – Can lead to hacked accounts.

How to Keep Your Child's Information Private

- **Set Social Media Accounts to Private** – Ensure only trusted friends can see posts.
- **Teach Kids to Think Before They Post** – Remind them that once something is online, it's hard to remove.
- **Use Nicknames for Gaming and Chat Apps** – Avoid using real names in public profiles.

- **Review Online Profiles Together** – Check and update security settings regularly.
- **Teach Password Safety** – Use strong passwords and never share them with friends.

Inappropriate Content: Exposure to Violence, Hate Speech, and Adult Content

The Risks of Inappropriate Content

Children may come across harmful content online without actively searching for it. This could include violent images, hate speech, extreme political views, and adult material. Exposure to such content can lead to fear, confusion, and even changes in behavior.

How Kids Encounter Inappropriate Content

- **Accidental Searches** – Simple misspellings in search engines can lead to harmful content.
- **Links from Friends** – Children may share shocking videos unknowingly.
- **Pop-up Ads and Clickbait** – Websites use misleading ads to attract clicks.
- **Video Recommendations** – Platforms like YouTube may autoplay inappropriate videos.

How to Shield Kids from Harmful Content

- **Enable Safe Browsing Filters** – Activate parental controls on search engines.

- **Use Kid-Friendly Platforms** – Allow younger children to use child-safe apps.
- **Talk About Internet Content** – Teach kids how to report inappropriate material.
- **Monitor Video and App Usage** – Check what they watch and play regularly.
- **Install Content Blockers** – Use filtering software to prevent access to harmful sites.

Scams and Phishing Attacks on Kids

Understanding Online Scams

Scammers target children because they are less likely to recognize fraud. These scams can steal money, access personal information, or trick kids into downloading harmful software.

Common Types of Online Scams

- **Fake Prizes and Giveaways** – "You've won a free iPhone! Click here!"
- **Gaming Scams** – "Get free in-game currency by entering your password!"
- **Phishing Emails** – Emails pretending to be from banks or popular websites.
- **Fake Friend Requests** – Strangers pretending to be peers to steal information.

How to Teach Kids to Avoid Scams

- **Never Click Suspicious Links** – Teach kids to avoid unknown links in emails or messages.
- **Check Website URLs** – Show them how to identify fake or scam websites.
- **Be Wary of 'Too Good to Be True' Offers** – If it sounds too good to be real, it probably is.
- **Report Suspicious Activity** – Teach them to report scams immediately.
- **Use Secure Payment Methods** – Ensure kids never enter payment details without parental approval.

Final Thoughts

Understanding these online threats is the first step in keeping your child safe. As digital parenting evolves, staying informed and engaged in your child's online life is more important than ever. By taking the right precautions, you can protect your child and ensure they have a positive and secure online experience.

Part 2: Monitoring & Supervising Your Child's Digital Life

Chapter 3: Setting Digital Boundaries for Kids

The internet is an incredible tool, offering unlimited opportunities for learning, creativity, and communication. However, without proper guidance and rules, it can also become a source of distraction, risk, and unhealthy habits for children. As a parent, it's essential to set clear digital boundaries to ensure your child develops a balanced and responsible approach to technology. In this chapter, we'll explore how to determine age-appropriate internet use, create a family digital agreement, set effective screen time limits, and encourage a healthy balance between online and offline activities.

Understanding Age-Appropriate Internet Use

Every child interacts with technology differently based on their age, cognitive abilities, and level of maturity. Understanding what is suitable for different age groups helps parents establish realistic expectations and protective measures.

Digital Use by Age Group

Toddlers (Ages 2-4):

- Limited exposure to digital screens, ideally under 30 minutes per day.
- Content should be highly educational and interactive, such as PBS Kids, ABCmouse, or CBeebies.
- Parental co-viewing is essential to help children understand and engage appropriately.

Young Children (Ages 5-7):

- Internet use should be monitored and limited to 1 hour per day.
- Only age-appropriate websites and educational games should be accessible.
- Introduction to basic digital safety concepts like asking permission before going online.

Older Children (Ages 8-12):

- Screen time can be extended to 1-2 hours a day, but a healthy mix of offline activities should be encouraged.
- Social media use is discouraged at this stage, though children may begin supervised online communication.
- Parental controls should be in place to restrict access to inappropriate content.
- Teach kids about privacy, such as not sharing personal information online.

Teenagers (Ages 13-18):

- Teens may require more screen time for schoolwork, social interactions, and hobbies, but limits should still be in place to prevent overuse.
- Open discussions about responsible social media use, cyberbullying, and online reputation should be frequent.
- Encourage self-regulation and accountability for screen time and digital interactions.

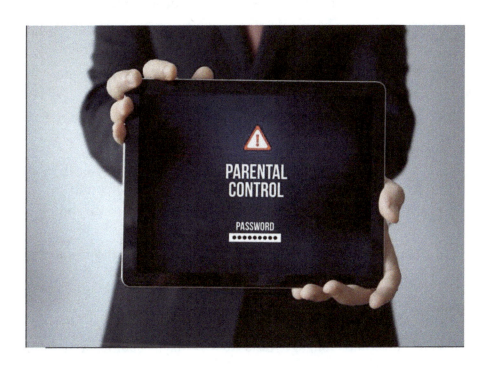

Creating a Family Digital Agreement

One of the most effective ways to set digital boundaries is by creating a **Family Digital Agreement**. This is a written or verbal contract that outlines the rules for internet and device use in your household. It ensures that children understand expectations, consequences, and safety measures while using technology.

Steps to Creating a Family Digital Agreement

Set Clear Expectations:

- Discuss appropriate and inappropriate online activities.
- Outline what websites, apps, and games are permitted.
- Specify screen-free zones, such as bedrooms or mealtimes.

Define Time Limits:

- Determine the maximum daily or weekly screen time allowance.
- Set designated screen time breaks to avoid digital fatigue.

Address Online Safety Rules:

- Teach kids never to share personal information online.
- Discuss the importance of reporting inappropriate content or messages.
- Establish rules about accepting friend requests from strangers.

Balance Online and Offline Activities:

- Ensure kids engage in outdoor play, reading, and family activities.
- Encourage alternative hobbies that don't involve screens.

Set Consequences for Rule-Breaking:

- Clearly outline consequences for violating digital rules (e.g., loss of privileges).

- Keep the enforcement fair and consistent.

Once the agreement is in place, **review it regularly** and **update it as needed** to match your child's evolving digital needs.

Establishing Screen Time Limits That Work

Excessive screen time can lead to sleep disturbances, reduced physical activity, and lower attention spans. Setting appropriate limits ensures children develop healthy habits while still enjoying the benefits of technology.

Tips for Effective Screen Time Management

Use Technology to Limit Technology:

- Set up parental controls and app timers on devices.
- Use apps like Google Family Link or Apple Screen Time to track usage.

Follow the "20-20-20 Rule":

- Every 20 minutes of screen time, encourage kids to look at something 20 feet away for at least 20 seconds to reduce eye strain.

Implement Screen-Free Zones and Times:

- No devices at the dinner table.
- No screens an hour before bedtime to promote better sleep.

Tie Screen Time to Responsibilities:

- Homework and chores must be completed before screen time is granted.
- Encourage "tech-free" family bonding activities like board games or nature walks.

Lead by Example:

- Parents should also set limits on their own screen time.
- Model good digital habits by prioritizing face-to-face interactions.
- Encouraging a Healthy Online-Offline Balance

While digital devices are an integral part of modern life, it's essential to teach children that life exists beyond screens. Encouraging an online-offline balance helps maintain physical, mental, and emotional well-being.

Ways to Promote a Balanced Lifestyle

Encourage Outdoor Play and Physical Activity:

- Plan daily activities that require movement, such as sports, hiking, or cycling.
- Limit sedentary time by encouraging breaks between screen use.

Prioritize Face-to-Face Socialization:

- Encourage kids to spend time with friends and family in real life.
- Promote hobbies that involve in-person interactions, like music lessons or team sports.

Schedule Device-Free Family Time:

- Have a weekly game night or family outing without screens.
- Make bedtime a screen-free period to promote better sleep habits.

Encourage Creative Screen Time Use:

- Instead of passive scrolling, guide kids toward creative activities like coding, digital art, or video editing.
- Balance entertainment (gaming, videos) with productive screen use (educational content, online learning).

Teach Time Management Skills:

- Help kids create a daily schedule that includes a mix of schoolwork, outdoor activities, and relaxation.
- Encourage time-blocking techniques to balance screen use with other priorities.

By setting clear digital boundaries, families can foster responsible tech use, prevent digital addiction, and create a safer, healthier online experience for children. Start today by having an open discussion with your child, setting rules together, and consistently reinforcing them for long-term success.

Chapter 4: Parental Controls & Monitoring Tools

Setting Up Parental Controls on Devices and Apps

Understanding Parental Controls

Parental controls are tools that allow parents to manage, filter, and monitor their child's online activities. These settings help protect children from inappropriate content, limit screen time, and prevent unauthorized purchases or downloads. While no system is foolproof, using parental controls creates a safer digital environment for kids and helps enforce household rules for online behavior.

Parental controls can be set up on different levels:

- **Device-Level Controls** – Settings applied directly to smartphones, tablets, computers, and gaming consoles.
- **App-Specific Controls** – Individual apps like YouTube, TikTok, and Netflix offer their own parental restrictions.
- **Network-Level Controls** – Some internet providers allow parental controls at the router level, filtering content for all devices on the home network.

How to Set Up Parental Controls on Various Devices

Smartphones and Tablets

Most modern smartphones and tablets come with built-in parental controls that allow parents to manage what children can access and how long they can use their devices.

For iOS (iPhone & iPad):

- Open **Settings** and tap **Screen Time**.
- Tap **Turn On Screen Time** and follow the prompts to set it up.
- Tap **Content & Privacy Restrictions** and enable the toggle.
- Customize settings for:
  - **App Limits** – Restrict usage time for certain apps.
  - **Content Restrictions** – Block adult content, movies, or apps based on age ratings.
  - **Purchases** – Prevent unauthorized in-app purchases.

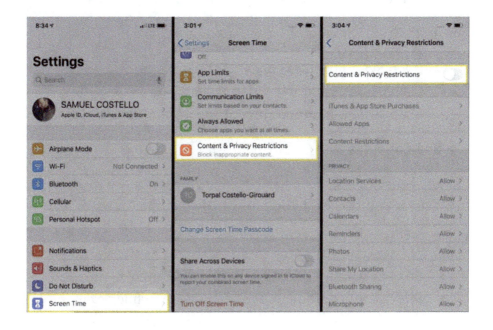

For Android Devices:

- Open **Settings** and navigate to **Digital Wellbeing & Parental Controls**.
- Tap **Parental Controls** and follow the prompts to set up supervision.
- Use **Google Family Link** to manage your child's app usage, screen time, and content restrictions remotely.

Computers and Laptops

For Windows:

- Go to **Settings > Accounts > Family & other users**.
- Click **Add a family member** and create a child account.

- Configure restrictions via **Microsoft Family Safety**.

For macOS:

- Open **System Preferences > Screen Time**.
- Click **Options** and select **Use Screen Time Passcode**.
- Enable restrictions on content, websites, and downloads.

Gaming Consoles

Gaming consoles also have parental control features to restrict game time and prevent access to mature-rated content.

For PlayStation:

- Go to **Settings > Family & Parental Controls**.
- Select **Family Management** and create a child account.
- Apply restrictions to limit playtime and purchases.

For Xbox:

- Open **Settings > Account > Family settings**.
- Set up restrictions for game ratings, communication, and screen time.

For Nintendo Switch:

- Download the **Nintendo Parental Controls** app.
- Link the console and adjust settings for game time limits and content filtering.

How to Use Built-in Safety Features (YouTube, Google, iOS, Android)

YouTube Safety Features

YouTube contains a vast range of content, including videos that may not be appropriate for children. Parents can enable restrictions to make YouTube a safer platform.

How to Enable YouTube Restricted Mode:

- Open the YouTube app or website.
- Tap the **Profile Icon** and go to **Settings**.
- Scroll to **Restricted Mode** and turn it on.

For younger children, **YouTube Kids** is a better alternative with pre-filtered content appropriate for kids under 12.

Google SafeSearch

Google's **SafeSearch** filters explicit content from search results, making it an essential tool for kids using the internet.

How to Enable SafeSearch on Google:

- Open Google and go to **Settings > Search Settings**.
- Scroll to **SafeSearch Filters** and enable it.
- iOS and Android Safety Features
- Both iOS and Android have built-in tools to help parents manage their child's digital habits.

For iOS:

- Use **Screen Time** to limit app usage and block content.
- Enable **Find My iPhone** to track your child's location.

For Android:

- Use **Google Family Link** for supervision.
- Set up **Safe Browsing** in Chrome to prevent access to dangerous websites.

Monitoring Apps: The Pros and Cons

Many third-party monitoring apps offer more extensive tracking features beyond built-in parental controls. However, these apps come with advantages and disadvantages.

Pros of Monitoring Apps

- **Detailed Activity Reports** – See which apps, websites, and messages your child interacts with.
- **Location Tracking** – Track your child's real-time location for safety.
- **App Blocking** – Prevent access to inappropriate or excessive screen time apps.
- **Time Management** – Set daily limits for specific apps and devices.

Cons of Monitoring Apps

- **Privacy Concerns** – Over-monitoring can harm trust between parents and children.
- **False Sense of Security** – No tool is 100% effective at preventing online risks.
- **Tech-Savvy Kids May Bypass Restrictions** – Older children may find ways to disable or circumvent monitoring tools.

Popular monitoring apps include **Bark, Qustodio, Net Nanny, and Norton Family**.

Tracking Online Activity Without Violating Trust

Balancing Supervision and Respect

While it's important to keep kids safe online, excessive monitoring can lead to feelings of mistrust. The best approach is **open communication combined with supervision**.

Tips for Tracking Without Being Overbearing

- **Be Transparent** – Let your child know you have monitoring tools in place.
- **Set Clear Expectations** – Explain the reasons behind parental controls.
- **Encourage Open Conversations** – Foster an environment where kids feel comfortable discussing their online experiences.
- **Use Collaborative Tools** – Instead of secretly tracking, involve children in setting up safety measures together.

- **Adjust Controls as They Grow** – As kids mature, provide more online independence while keeping core safety features active.

Conclusion

Parental controls and monitoring tools are essential for keeping children safe online, but they must be used thoughtfully. The goal is not to spy on kids but to guide them toward responsible digital habits. By setting up the right controls, using built-in safety features, and maintaining open communication, parents can create a safe and supportive online environment for their children.

Chapter 5: Safe Social Media and Messaging Practices

The digital world has transformed how children and teens interact with others. Social media platforms and messaging apps allow them to stay connected, express themselves, and explore various interests. However, these platforms also come with risks such as privacy concerns, cyberbullying, scams, and exposure to harmful content.

As a parent, understanding these platforms and teaching your child safe practices is essential. This chapter will guide you through the most popular social media platforms, how to set privacy restrictions, how to recognize fake accounts and scams, and how to prevent cyberbullying.

Popular Social Media Platforms (Instagram, Snapchat, TikTok, Discord)

Why Understanding These Platforms is Important

Social media is a significant part of many children's daily lives. They use these platforms to communicate with friends, watch videos, share updates, and join online communities. However, not all social media platforms are designed with children's safety in mind. Some apps have strict privacy controls, while others expose children to potential dangers, including online predators and harmful content.

Below are four of the most commonly used social media platforms among children and teens, along with their key features and risks.

1. Instagram

What It Is: Instagram is a photo and video-sharing platform that allows users to post pictures, create stories, and engage with others through comments and direct messages.

Potential Risks:

- Public profiles can expose children to strangers.
- Direct messaging allows unsolicited contact.
- Cyberbullying through comments and messages.
- Exposure to unrealistic beauty standards and harmful content.

2. Snapchat

What It Is: Snapchat is a messaging app that allows users to send photos and videos that disappear after being viewed.

Potential Risks:

- Messages disappear, making it harder for parents to monitor conversations.
- "Snap Map" shows a user's location in real time.
- Friends lists can include strangers if not managed carefully.

3. TikTok

What It Is: TikTok is a short-form video platform where users can create, watch, and engage with videos.

Potential Risks:

- Public videos can attract unwanted attention.
- Comments sections can be a space for bullying.
- Exposure to inappropriate challenges or dangerous trends.

4. Discord

What It Is: Discord is a messaging platform popular among gamers, allowing users to join servers and chat via text, voice, or video.

Potential Risks:

- Open servers allow strangers to communicate with children.
- Direct messaging is unfiltered unless settings are changed.
- Exposure to explicit or inappropriate content in public groups.

What Parents Can Do:

- Familiarize yourself with the platforms your child uses.
- Encourage open discussions about online interactions.
- Set up parental controls and privacy settings.

Setting Privacy Settings and Restrictions

Why Privacy Settings Matter

Privacy settings are the first layer of protection for children using social media. When properly configured, they help control who can see your child's content, who can contact them, and what personal information is shared.

Steps to Set Privacy Controls

- **Switch to Private Accounts**: Most platforms allow users to choose between public and private accounts. Private accounts limit visibility to approved followers only.
- **Restrict Messaging**: Disable direct messaging from strangers. On platforms like Instagram and Discord, ensure that only approved friends can send messages.
- **Turn Off Location Sharing**: Features like Snapchat's Snap Map should be disabled to prevent sharing a child's location.
- **Limit Comments and Mentions**: Most platforms allow users to control who can comment on their posts and mention them in content.
- **Regularly Review Friend Lists**: Encourage children to only accept friend requests from people they know personally.
- **Enable Content Filters**: TikTok, Instagram, and YouTube have content restriction settings that filter out explicit or harmful material.

What Parents Can Do:

- Periodically check privacy settings with your child.
- Discuss the importance of keeping personal information private.
- Remind them not to share passwords or login details with friends.

Teaching Kids to Recognize Fake Accounts and Scams

How Fake Accounts and Scams Target Kids

Fake accounts are often used to trick children into sharing personal information, clicking harmful links, or engaging in inappropriate conversations. These accounts can appear as friendly peers, influencers, or even gaming partners.

Signs of a Fake Account

- **No Profile Picture or Generic Photos**: Fake profiles often lack personal pictures or use stock images.
- **Few Posts or No Activity**: Scammers typically create new accounts with little real engagement.
- **Requests for Personal Information**: Legitimate friends won't ask for passwords, personal details, or money.
- **Too-Good-To-Be-True Offers**: Scams often include fake giveaways or rewards for clicking a suspicious link.
- **Suspicious Direct Messages**: Messages from unknown users that ask for personal information or try to move conversations to another app.

How Kids Can Stay Safe

- **Never Accept Friend Requests from Strangers**.
- **Avoid Clicking on Unverified Links**.
- **Report Suspicious Accounts** to the platform immediately.
- **Trust Their Instincts**: If something feels off, they should talk to a trusted adult.

How to Spot and Prevent Cyberbullying

Understanding Cyberbullying

Cyberbullying occurs when someone uses digital platforms to harass, intimidate, or humiliate others. It can take many forms, including hurtful comments, spreading false rumors, or even threats.

Common Signs of Cyberbullying

- A child suddenly avoids social media or messaging apps.
- Emotional distress after using their phone or computer.
- Reluctance to talk about online experiences.

- Sudden changes in mood, sleep, or appetite.

Preventing Cyberbullying

- **Encourage Open Communication**: Let children know they can talk to you about any negative online experiences.
- **Teach Responsible Online Behavior**: Encourage kindness and respect in digital interactions.
- **Use the Block and Report Features**: Social media platforms provide tools to block bullies and report harmful behavior.
- **Monitor Online Activity Without Invading Privacy**: Maintain trust while keeping an eye on concerning interactions.
- **Encourage a Healthy Relationship with Social Media**: Remind kids that they are in control of their digital environment and can step away if needed.

What Parents Can Do If Their Child is Being Cyberbullied

- **Stay Calm and Supportive**: Encourage them to talk about their experience.
- **Document the Bullying**: Take screenshots before reporting the behavior.
- **Report the User**: Use platform tools to report cyberbullies.
- **Seek Professional Help if Necessary**: A counselor or therapist can help if the bullying affects their mental health.

Conclusion

Social media can be a wonderful way for children to connect, learn, and express themselves. However, it also comes with risks that require parental guidance. By understanding popular platforms, setting strong privacy controls, recognizing fake accounts and scams, and preventing cyberbullying, you can help your child have a safe and positive online experience.

Encourage open conversations, educate your child about potential dangers, and empower them to make smart choices. With the right knowledge and tools, digital parenting becomes a manageable and rewarding journey.

Part 3: Educating and Empowering Your Child

Chapter 6: Teaching Kids About Online Safety

The internet is an incredible tool that opens doors to education, entertainment, and social connections. However, just as in the real world, children must learn how to navigate the online world safely. Parents play a crucial role in preparing their kids for the digital landscape by teaching them how to recognize risks, handle threats, and think critically about online content. This chapter will guide you through the best ways to approach online safety conversations with your child, ensuring they feel informed and empowered rather than fearful or overwhelmed.

Teach Your Kids About

- ✓ The dangers of the internet
- ✓ How to protect your identity
- ✓ Creating strong passwords
- ✓ Not engaging with strangers in person or online
- ✓ Keeping social media accounts private
- ✓ Being careful about what they post

The Right Way to Talk About Internet Dangers

Discussing online risks with children can be tricky. You don't want to scare them, but you also need to ensure they understand the potential dangers. The key is to approach these conversations with an open and reassuring tone, making them feel safe and supported rather than anxious or afraid.

Step 1: Create an Open and Ongoing Conversation

The best way to educate kids about online safety is to make it a regular part of their lives. Instead of sitting them down for one big talk, integrate discussions naturally into everyday situations. If they mention a new app or social media trend, use that as an opportunity to talk about privacy, safe interactions, or misinformation.

Step 2: Use Age-Appropriate Language

Children of different ages have different levels of understanding. Keep your explanations simple and relatable. For younger kids, you might compare online safety to crossing the street—just like they look both ways before stepping onto the road, they should pause and think before clicking on a link or talking to someone online. For older kids, discussions can involve more complex topics like data privacy and cyber threats.

Step 3: Focus on Safety, Not Fear

While it's important to highlight potential dangers, your goal should be to empower your child with knowledge, not to scare them into avoiding technology altogether. Instead of saying, "The internet is full of dangerous people," say, "There are some people online who might not be who they say they are, so it's important to be cautious."

Step 4: Encourage Questions and Honesty

Let your child know they can always come to you if something makes them uncomfortable online. Praise them for asking questions or reporting a problem rather than making them feel like they've done something wrong. A child who fears punishment may hide their online activities, which can make them more vulnerable.

Teaching Kids to Identify and Handle Cyberbullying

Cyberbullying is one of the biggest risks children face online. Unlike traditional bullying, cyberbullying can follow a child home through social media, messaging apps, and online games. Teaching kids how to recognize, respond to, and prevent cyberbullying is essential for their digital well-being.

Step 1: Help Them Recognize Cyberbullying

Explain that cyberbullying includes any mean, harmful, or threatening behavior that happens through digital platforms. Some common forms include:

- Spreading rumors or lies about someone online.
- Posting embarrassing photos or videos without consent.
- Sending mean or threatening messages.
- Excluding someone from online groups or activities.
- Creating fake profiles to harass or impersonate someone.

Step 2: Teach Them How to Respond

If your child encounters cyberbullying, they should:

- **Not respond to the bully.** Reacting can make the situation worse.
- **Save the evidence.** Encourage them to take screenshots of the messages or posts.
- **Block and report the bully.** Most platforms have options to block and report abusive behavior.

- **Talk to a trusted adult.** Whether it's you, a teacher, or another trusted adult, they should know they don't have to handle it alone.

Step 3: Encourage Kindness and Positive Online Behavior

Help your child understand that their actions also impact others. Encourage them to:

- Think before they post.
- Speak up if they see someone else being bullied.
- Be kind and supportive online, just as they would in person.

How to Talk About Online Predators Without Scaring Them

One of the most concerning aspects of online safety is protecting children from predators. However, this conversation must be handled carefully to avoid unnecessary fear while ensuring children recognize and respond appropriately to suspicious interactions.

Step 1: Explain the Concept in a Simple Way

Tell your child that, just like in real life, not everyone online is who they claim to be. Some people might pretend to be kids or friendly adults but have bad intentions. Let them know that if someone online ever asks them to keep a secret, tries to be overly friendly, or asks for personal information, they should stop the conversation immediately and tell a trusted adult.

Step 2: Set Clear Guidelines for Online Interactions

To keep kids safe, establish rules such as:

- Never sharing personal details (name, school, address, phone number) with strangers online.
- Avoiding direct messages from unknown people.
- Never agreeing to meet someone from the internet in real life.
- Reporting any suspicious messages immediately.

Step 3: Teach Them How to Respond to Uncomfortable Situations

If a stranger online starts asking personal questions or makes them feel uncomfortable, they should:

- **Stop responding immediately.**
- **Take screenshots if necessary.**
- **Block the person and report the account.**
- **Tell a trusted adult right away.**

Encouraging Critical Thinking About Online Content

Not everything on the internet is true, and children must learn to think critically about the content they see online. Whether it's a viral challenge, fake news, or misleading advertisements, teaching kids to question and analyze information is key to their online safety.

Step 1: Teach Them to Ask Questions

Encourage your child to think critically by asking:

- **Who created this content?**
- **Is it from a reliable source?**
- **What is the purpose—information, entertainment, or manipulation?**
- **Are there multiple sources confirming this information?**

Step 2: Explain the Dangers of Fake News and Misinformation

Show examples of fake news and explain how it spreads. Help them understand that just because something appears in a video or article doesn't mean it's true. Teach them how to fact-check using trusted sources.

Step 3: Discuss Online Trends and Challenges

Many online challenges go viral, but some can be dangerous. Encourage your child to think before participating in any trend by asking themselves:

- Could this harm me or someone else?
- Would I still do this if no one was watching?
- Why am I really doing this?

Final Thoughts

Teaching children about online safety is an ongoing process. By fostering open communication, setting clear guidelines, and encouraging critical thinking, you can help your child navigate the internet with confidence and caution. Remember, the goal is not to instill fear but to equip them with the knowledge and skills they need to stay safe online.

Encourage your child to talk to you about their online experiences, good or bad, and remind them that they are never alone when facing digital challenges. By working together, you can create a safe and positive online experience for your family.

Chapter 7: Digital Footprint & Online Reputation

What Is a Digital Footprint?

Every time we use the internet, we leave behind traces of our activity. These traces form what is known as a **digital footprint**. Simply put, a digital footprint is the collection of information about a person that exists online due to their internet usage. This can include social media posts, comments, likes, shares, search history, online purchases, and even deleted content that may still be stored somewhere on the internet.

There are two main types of digital footprints:

- **Active Digital Footprint** – This consists of data that a person **deliberately** shares online. For example, posting photos on social media, writing blog posts, or engaging in online discussions.
- **Passive Digital Footprint** – This includes information collected **without the user's direct knowledge**. For instance, websites tracking user activity, cookies saving browsing history, or companies collecting user data for advertising.

Most kids today don't realize that everything they do online contributes to their digital footprint. They may think a deleted post is gone forever, but in reality, it may have been archived, screenshotted, or saved elsewhere. This is why it is essential to educate children about **how their online actions create a lasting presence on the internet**.

How Kids' Online Actions Affect Their Future

A child's digital footprint may seem harmless when they are young, but it can significantly impact their future. In today's world, schools, employers, and even sports teams **often check a person's online presence** before making decisions about scholarships, admissions, or job offers.

Here's how online actions can influence a child's future:

- **College Admissions** – Many universities check applicants' social media pages to see if they reflect responsible behavior. A single inappropriate post or offensive comment could harm their chances of getting accepted.
- **Job Opportunities** – Employers frequently conduct online background checks. If a child has shared controversial or reckless content, it might create a negative impression when they apply for a job in the future.
- **Scholarships and Internships** – Organizations offering scholarships often assess a student's character through their online presence. A responsible, positive digital footprint can improve their chances, while an irresponsible one can have the opposite effect.
- **Reputation and Relationships** – A child's online actions can influence how peers, teachers, and future colleagues perceive them. Negative behavior, such as cyberbullying, inappropriate

humor, or offensive comments, can lead to **long-term social and professional consequences**.

Children need to understand that the internet **never truly forgets**, and the things they post today can shape their future opportunities. Helping them build a positive digital footprint is a critical aspect of responsible digital parenting.

The Risks of Posting Personal Information

Many children and teenagers freely share personal details online without realizing the potential risks. Posting personal information can lead to **privacy breaches, identity theft, cyberbullying, and even physical danger**.

Dangers of Sharing Personal Details

- **Identity Theft** – Cybercriminals can use details like full names, birthdays, addresses, and school names to steal identities, create fake accounts, or commit fraud.
- **Cyberstalking and Predators** – Posting locations, daily routines, or personal photos can make it easier for online predators or strangers to track and target children.
- **Hacked Accounts** – Sharing too much information makes it easier for hackers to guess passwords, security questions, or gain access to private accounts.
- **Embarrassment and Regret** – Sometimes, children post things impulsively, such as personal thoughts, private messages, or embarrassing pictures. These can resurface years later and cause regret.

- **Misuse of Information** – Even seemingly harmless posts can be **edited, taken out of context, or used against** a child in the future.

How to Protect Personal Information Online

- **Use Privacy Settings** – Teach kids to adjust privacy settings on social media to control who can see their posts.
- **Avoid Posting Full Names and Locations** – Encourage children to **never** share personal details like their full name, school name, or home address publicly.
- **Think Before Sharing** – Before posting, ask: "Would I be okay if a stranger saw this?" If the answer is no, it's better not to post.
- **Be Careful with Photos** – Even innocent pictures can contain hidden details, like school uniforms or house addresses, that can be used to identify locations.
- **Limit Social Media Friends** – Accepting friend requests from strangers increases the risk of data exposure. Encourage kids to only connect with people they know in real life.

By teaching kids to be mindful of what they share, parents can help them avoid serious consequences and keep their personal information secure.

Teaching Kids to Think Before They Share

Helping children develop **good judgment** about what to share online is crucial for building a positive and safe digital presence. Since young minds act impulsively, they may post things **without considering the long-term impact**.

The "THINK" Before You Post Method

A simple way to teach kids responsible online behavior is to follow the THINK method. Before posting, they should ask themselves:

- **T – Is it True?** → Is the information factual, or could it spread false or misleading content?
- **H – Is it Helpful?** → Does it add value, help others, or create a positive impact?
- **I – Is it Inspiring?** → Does it encourage kindness, positivity, or meaningful conversation?
- **N – Is it Necessary?** → Does this information need to be shared, or is it better kept private?
- **K – Is it Kind?** → Would this post hurt someone's feelings or create negativity?

If a post doesn't pass this checklist, then it's better **not** to share it.

Steps to Teach Responsible Sharing

- **Have Open Conversations** – Regularly discuss the importance of thinking before sharing online. Ask kids how they would feel if their posts were seen by a teacher, future employer, or grandparent.
- **Use Real-Life Examples** – Show them stories of people who faced consequences because of careless online posts. These real-world examples make the lesson more impactful.

- **Encourage Private Journaling** – If a child wants to express feelings, suggest **writing them in a journal instead of posting online**. This helps them process emotions safely.
- **Teach About Online Permanence** – Remind kids that screenshots, archives, and digital backups can make even deleted content accessible forever.
- **Lead by Example** – Children learn from their parents. Model responsible sharing by being mindful of your own online posts and behaviors.

By teaching kids to pause and think before they post, parents can guide them toward a **safe, responsible, and positive digital footprint**.

Final Thoughts

A child's **digital footprint shapes their future**. Whether it's college admissions, job opportunities, or personal reputation, everything they share online leaves an impact. By educating children about **what a digital footprint is, the risks of oversharing, and how to think before posting**, parents can empower them to make smart choices in the online world. Digital parenting isn't about restricting kids—it's about teaching them to **navigate the internet wisely and safely**.

With the right guidance, kids can build a **positive online reputation** that will benefit them for years to come.

Chapter 8: Safe Online Gaming for Kids

Gaming has become one of the most popular activities among children today. Whether it's playing on a console, PC, tablet, or smartphone, online games provide entertainment, social interaction, and even learning opportunities. However, as fun as gaming can be, it also comes with risks that parents must understand and address. This chapter will guide you through the challenges of online gaming and help you create a safe gaming environment for your child.

The Risks of Online Gaming (Chat Rooms, Microtransactions, Addiction)

1. Online Chat Rooms and Unmonitored Communication

Many online games include chat features that allow players to communicate with one another. While this can be great for teamwork and making friends, it also opens the door to potential dangers such as:

- **Exposure to strangers:** Children may interact with unknown players who could have bad intentions.
- **Inappropriate conversations:** Some players use online chat to spread harmful content, bullying, or offensive language.

- **Privacy risks:** Kids may unknowingly share personal information, like their real name, location, or school, making them vulnerable to online predators.

To minimize these risks, parents should ensure that:

- **Chat settings are restricted** to friends and known contacts.
- **Voice chat is disabled** or monitored, depending on the child's age.
- **Children understand online etiquette** and know how to report harmful behavior.

2. Microtransactions and In-Game Purchases

Many games include **in-app purchases**, which allow players to buy virtual items such as costumes, weapons, or in-game currency. The dangers of microtransactions include:

- **Unexpected expenses:** Kids may unknowingly spend real money on in-game purchases.
- **Gambling-like mechanics:** Loot boxes and random rewards can encourage addictive spending behaviors.
- **Peer pressure:** Friends might persuade children to buy certain in-game items to fit in.

To protect your child:

- **Disable or password-protect in-game purchases.**
- **Educate them on responsible spending.** Explain the difference between virtual money and real money.
- **Set up a spending limit or allowance** if purchases are allowed.

3. Gaming Addiction and Excessive Screen Time

Some children become so immersed in gaming that it affects their daily lives. Signs of gaming addiction include:

- **Neglecting schoolwork or responsibilities** due to excessive gaming.
- **Irritability or frustration** when they can't play.
- **Skipping meals or losing sleep** because of late-night gaming sessions.

To prevent gaming addiction:

- **Establish a daily gaming time limit** and ensure a balance between gaming and other activities.
- **Encourage alternative hobbies,** such as sports, reading, or outdoor play.
- **Use parental controls** to enforce playtime restrictions.

Setting Boundaries for Safe Gaming

As a parent, setting clear gaming rules will help your child enjoy games responsibly. Here's how you can do it:

1. Create a Family Gaming Agreement

A family gaming agreement sets expectations for gaming time, content, and behavior. This should include:

- **Allowed gaming hours** (e.g., 1 hour on school nights, 2 hours on weekends).

- **Where gaming is permitted** (e.g., in the living room rather than alone in the bedroom).
- **What types of games are allowed** based on age-appropriate content.

2. Encourage Open Communication

Ensure your child feels comfortable discussing their gaming experiences with you. Ask questions like:

- "What games are you playing?"
- "Who do you talk to in the game?"
- "Have you seen anything that made you uncomfortable?"

3. Use Parental Controls

Most gaming platforms allow parents to:

- **Set time limits on playtime.**
- **Restrict purchases and in-game spending.**
- **Filter inappropriate content or disable chat functions.**

Recognizing and Avoiding In-Game Scams and Predators

1. Common In-Game Scams

Scammers target young players in online games, often tricking them into giving away valuable items or personal details. Some common scams include:

- **Fake giveaways:** Scammers promise free items in exchange for login details.
- **Phishing links:** Messages disguised as game updates or special offers that steal personal information.
- **Account theft:** Someone posing as a game administrator requesting passwords.

How to Protect Your Child:

- Teach them **never to share login information** with anyone, even friends.
- Show them how to **identify suspicious messages and report scammers.**
- Enable **two-factor authentication** to secure accounts.

2. Online Predators in Gaming

- Some predators use gaming platforms to build trust with children. They may:
- Pretend to be another child to form friendships.
- Try to move conversations to private messaging apps.
- Pressure children into sharing photos or personal details.

Safety Measures:

- Monitor who your child interacts with online.
- Keep gaming consoles and computers in shared spaces.
- Teach children to block and report suspicious players.

Selecting Age-Appropriate Games

Not all games are suitable for children. Some contain violence, strong language, or mature themes. Here's how to choose the right games:

1. Check Game Ratings

Most games have an **ESRB (Entertainment Software Rating Board) rating** that indicates the appropriate age group:

- **E (Everyone):** Suitable for all ages.
- **E10+ (Everyone 10 and older):** May contain mild violence or language.
- **T (Teen 13+):** Contains more intense action, suggestive themes, or mild blood.
- **M (Mature 17+):** Includes violence, strong language, or adult themes.

2. Read Reviews and Watch Gameplay Videos

Before allowing your child to play a game, check:

- **Online reviews and parent forums** to see if the game is safe.
- **YouTube gameplay videos** to get an idea of the content.
- **Parental control settings** that can adjust in-game features.

3. Choose Games That Encourage Learning and Creativity

Some games are not only fun but also educational. Consider:

- **Puzzle and logic games** (e.g., Minecraft, Portal, Scribblenauts).
- **Strategy games** that develop problem-solving skills (e.g., Civilization, SimCity).

- **Co-op games** that encourage teamwork (e.g., Lego games, Mario Kart).

Conclusion

Online gaming can be an exciting and rewarding experience for children when done safely. By understanding the risks, setting clear boundaries, recognizing scams, and selecting age-appropriate games, parents can create a safe gaming environment. Encourage open discussions with your child and stay involved in their gaming world. With the right guidance, gaming can be a positive and enjoyable part of their life.

By following the strategies in this chapter, you can ensure that your child enjoys the best aspects of online gaming while staying protected from its dangers.

Part 4: Protecting Your Child from Cyber Threats

Chapter 9: Cybersecurity Basics for Families

The internet is a vast and powerful tool that connects people, provides knowledge, and offers entertainment. However, it also comes with risks, especially for children who may not fully understand online security. As a parent, it's essential to equip your family with the knowledge and habits needed to stay safe in the digital world. In this chapter, we will cover the core cybersecurity practices that every family should follow to ensure safe internet use.

Creating Strong Passwords and Using Two-Factor Authentication

Understanding the Importance of Strong Passwords

Passwords act as the first line of defense against hackers. A weak password is like leaving the front door of your home unlocked, making it easy for intruders to get in. Cybercriminals use various tactics, such as guessing common passwords or using automated tools to crack weak ones. This is why every online account, especially those used by children, must have a strong and unique password.

How to Create a Strong Password

To make your passwords more secure, follow these guidelines:

- **Use at least 12 characters** – The longer, the better.
- **Include a mix of uppercase and lowercase letters** – This increases complexity.
- **Use numbers and special characters** – Adding symbols (#, $, %, @) makes passwords harder to guess.
- **Avoid common words and phrases** – Do not use names, birthdays, or simple words like "password123."
- **Use a passphrase** – A sentence like "MyDogLovesToRunFast!" is easier to remember and more secure.
- **Never reuse passwords** – If one account is compromised, others could be at risk.

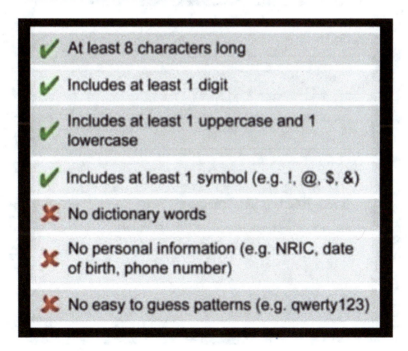

Using a Password Manager

Remembering unique passwords for every account can be challenging. A **password manager** is a tool that securely stores and generates strong passwords for you. Many password managers also help with filling in login details automatically, making them both convenient and secure.

Enabling Two-Factor Authentication (2FA)

A strong password is a great start, but **Two-Factor Authentication (2FA)** adds an extra layer of security. With 2FA, even if someone gets hold of your password, they still need a second form of verification to access your account.

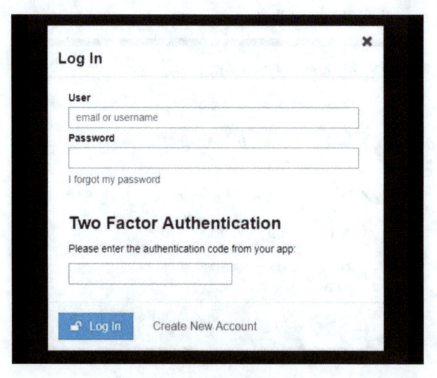

There are different types of 2FA, including:

- **Text message codes** – A one-time code is sent to your phone when logging in.
- **Authentication apps** – Apps like Google Authenticator or Authy generate codes without relying on SMS.
- **Biometric authentication** – Using fingerprints or facial recognition for added security.

Always enable 2FA on accounts that allow it, especially for banking, email, and social media.

Safe Browsing Practices for Kids

The Importance of Safe Browsing

Children are naturally curious and may accidentally click on harmful links, visit inappropriate websites, or download malicious software. Teaching them safe browsing habits will protect them from online threats and help them develop responsible internet use.

Tips for Safe Browsing

- **Use Kid-Friendly Search Engines** – Platforms like **Kiddle** or **YouTube Kids** filter out inappropriate content.
- **Activate Safe Search Settings** – Most browsers and search engines have a "Safe Search" feature to block explicit content.
- **Teach Kids to Identify Unsafe Websites** – Suspicious websites often have:
  - Poor design and excessive pop-ups
  - Strange web addresses (e.g., "freemovies123.xyz")
  - Fake security warnings
- **Encourage Kids to Ask Before Clicking** – If they receive unexpected links, they should always check with an adult.

- **Use Parental Controls and Content Filters** – Set up restrictions on browsers and devices to block harmful sites.
- **Importance of Logging Out and Clearing History**

Teach kids to **log out of accounts** after using shared devices. Additionally, encourage them to **clear their browsing history** when using public or shared computers to protect their privacy.

Avoiding Scams and Phishing Attacks

What Are Scams and Phishing?

Scammers try to trick people into giving away personal information, money, or access to their accounts. **Phishing** is one of the most common scams, where criminals send fake emails or messages pretending to be from a trusted company.

How to Recognize a Scam or Phishing Attempt

Suspicious Emails and Messages – Look for:

- Poor spelling and grammar
- Urgent or threatening language (e.g., "Your account will be deleted!")
- Unexpected attachments or links

Fake Websites – Scammers create sites that look like real ones to steal login details. Always check:

- The website address (legitimate sites use **https://**)
- Official logos and correct spellings

- **Too-Good-To-Be-True Offers** – If an online offer looks too perfect, it's probably a scam.
- **Requests for Personal Information** – Banks and companies **never** ask for passwords via email or text.

Teaching Kids to Avoid Online Scams

- **Never Click on Unknown Links** – Always verify links before clicking.
- **Don't Share Personal Information** – Teach kids to keep details like their full name, address, and school private.
- **Use Spam Filters** – Email providers have filters that help block scams.

How to Handle a Hacked Account

Signs That an Account Has Been Hacked

- You are **locked out** of an account, even with the correct password.
- You notice **unexpected activity**, such as new posts or messages you didn't send.
- Friends receive **suspicious messages** from your account.
- You get **alerts about logins from unknown locations.**

Steps to Take If an Account Is Hacked

- **Change Your Password Immediately** – Use a strong, new password that you haven't used before.

- **Enable Two-Factor Authentication** – If not already active, set it up.
- **Check Account Activity** – Look for any unauthorized changes, messages, or posts.
- **Log Out from All Devices** – Most platforms allow you to log out from all sessions.
- **Report the Hack to the Platform** – Contact customer support if you can't regain access.
- **Warn Family and Friends** – Let them know to ignore any suspicious messages.

Preventing Future Hacks

- **Keep software and apps updated** – Security updates help fix vulnerabilities.
- **Use different passwords for each account** – This prevents hackers from accessing multiple accounts if one password is stolen.
- **Be cautious with free Wi-Fi** – Avoid logging into important accounts on public networks.

Conclusion

Cybersecurity is not just about using strong passwords or enabling security features—it's about building awareness and practicing safe habits daily. By teaching your children about online threats and guiding them in responsible digital behavior, you can help protect them from cyber dangers. Encourage open discussions, set family rules for online safety, and always stay informed about the latest cybersecurity threats.

A well-protected family is a digitally empowered family!

Chapter 10: Dealing with Cyberbullying

The digital world offers many benefits for children, from education to entertainment and social connections. However, it also comes with risks, and one of the most serious threats children face online is **cyberbullying**. Unlike traditional bullying, which happens in person, cyberbullying takes place on social media, messaging apps, online forums, and gaming platforms. It can be just as harmful, if not more, because it follows children everywhere—even into their homes.

As a parent, knowing how to **identify, address, and prevent** cyberbullying is crucial in protecting your child's mental and emotional well-being. In this chapter, we will cover how to recognize the signs of cyberbullying, steps to take if your child is a victim, how to teach kids to respond, and when to escalate the issue to schools, social media platforms, or even law enforcement.

How to Spot Signs Your Child is Being Cyberbullied

Children often hesitate to tell their parents about cyberbullying due to fear, embarrassment, or worry that their online access will be taken away. This makes it important for parents to recognize warning signs on their own. Cyberbullying can take many forms, such as mean comments, spreading rumors, exclusion from online groups, threats, or even identity theft.

Behavioral and Emotional Signs

- **Sudden changes in mood** – Your child may seem unusually anxious, withdrawn, angry, or upset after using their phone or computer.
- **Loss of interest in online activities** – A child who previously enjoyed being online may suddenly avoid their favorite apps or games.
- **Avoidance of social situations** – They may start isolating themselves, avoiding friends, or hesitating to go to school.
- **Low self-esteem** – Increased self-criticism, negative self-talk, or expressing feelings of worthlessness can indicate they are struggling with online harassment.

Physical Signs

- **Changes in sleep patterns** – Difficulty sleeping, nightmares, or staying up late checking their phone.
- **Unexplained headaches or stomach aches** – Stress-related illnesses can be a result of cyberbullying.
- **Sudden changes in appetite** – Eating much less or more than usual.

Technology-Related Signs

- **Becoming secretive about their online activity** – Hiding their screen, changing passwords, or suddenly deleting accounts.

- **Receiving a high number of notifications but refusing to check them** – They may feel overwhelmed by mean comments or messages.
- **Blocking or unfriending people frequently** – While blocking is a good response, excessive blocking may indicate ongoing harassment.

If you notice these signs, it's important to **talk to your child in a calm and supportive manner** to understand what they are experiencing.

Steps to Take if Your Child is a Victim

If you confirm that your child is being cyberbullied, it's important to take action immediately. Here's a step-by-step approach to ensure their safety and emotional well-being.

Step 1: Stay Calm and Supportive

Your first reaction is crucial. Avoid overreacting, blaming, or showing panic, as this may make your child less likely to open up. Instead:

- Reassure them that they are not at fault.
- Express empathy and acknowledge their feelings.
- Let them know you will work together to find a solution.

Step 2: Gather Evidence

Before taking action, collect proof of the cyberbullying:

- **Take screenshots** of harmful messages, posts, or comments.
- **Save chat logs** from messaging apps.
- **Record the dates and times** when the bullying occurred.

- **Keep copies** of any threats or harmful content.

Step 3: Block and Report the Bully

Encourage your child to block the person bullying them and report the behavior through the platform's built-in reporting system. Most social media and gaming platforms have strict policies against cyberbullying.

Step 4: Strengthen Privacy Settings

- Adjust your child's privacy settings to limit who can contact them online. This includes:
- Restricting messages to only friends or approved contacts.
- Enabling content filters to block harmful messages.
- Turning off location sharing to protect their safety.

Step 5: Monitor Your Child's Emotional Health

Cyberbullying can take a toll on a child's mental well-being. If they show signs of severe distress, anxiety, or depression, consider seeking help from a school counselor or therapist.

Teaching Kids to Respond to Online Harassment

While parents can take preventive measures, children also need to be equipped with skills to handle cyberbullying on their own.

1. Ignore and Avoid Responding to Bullies

Explain to your child that responding with anger or retaliation often makes the situation worse. Many cyberbullies seek attention and reactions, so ignoring them can sometimes be the best strategy.

2. Use the "STOP" Approach

Teach your child this simple method:

- **S**ave the evidence.
- **T**ell a trusted adult.
- **O**nline safety settings should be checked.
- **P**rotect personal information.

3. Report the Bullying

Encourage them to use platform reporting tools to flag harmful content. Many sites allow you to report bullying anonymously.

4. Build Confidence and Resilience

Help your child develop confidence by encouraging positive self-talk and reminding them of their strengths. Role-play different responses so they feel prepared if bullying happens again.

When to Report Cyberbullying (to Schools, Platforms, Law Enforcement)

Some cases of cyberbullying need more than just parental intervention. Knowing when to escalate the situation is key to ensuring your child's safety.

1. Reporting to Schools

If the bullying involves classmates or happens on school-related platforms, inform school officials. Schools often have anti-bullying policies and can mediate conflicts.

2. Reporting to Social Media Platforms

Most social media sites have strict rules against cyberbullying. You can report:

- Offensive posts and comments.
- Harassing private messages.
- Fake accounts impersonating your child.

3. Reporting to Law Enforcement

In severe cases, cyberbullying may break the law. Contact local authorities if:

- Threats of violence are made.
- Explicit or illegal content is involved.
- Your child is being stalked or blackmailed online.

Final Thoughts

Cyberbullying is a serious issue, but parents can play a powerful role in protecting their children. By staying informed, creating open communication, and teaching kids how to handle online harassment, you can empower them to navigate the digital world safely. If your child experiences cyberbullying, take immediate action while offering them emotional support. Together, you can create a safer and healthier online experience for them.

Chapter 11: Protecting Kids from Online Predators

The internet has opened up a world of opportunities for learning, communication, and entertainment, but it has also introduced risks that parents must be aware of. One of the most serious threats children face online is the danger posed by online predators. These individuals use the anonymity of the internet to exploit children, often by building trust and manipulating them into unsafe situations. As a parent, understanding how predators operate, recognizing warning signs, and taking proactive steps to protect your child is crucial.

This chapter will help you identify how predators lure children, recognize changes in your child's behavior that may indicate a problem, take immediate steps if you suspect online grooming, and report suspicious activity to the appropriate authorities.

How Predators Lure Kids Online

Online predators use sophisticated and deceptive tactics to gain a child's trust before exploiting them. They often approach children through social media, gaming platforms, chat rooms, or direct messaging apps. Here are some of the most common ways they lure kids online:

1. **Building Trust Through Friendship**

- Predators often pose as children or teenagers to befriend young users. They may:
- Use fake profiles with appealing photos and interests that match the child's.
- Spend weeks or even months building a connection by talking about hobbies, school, or family life.
- Make the child feel understood and valued, especially if the child feels lonely or isolated.

2. **Flattery and Attention**

Children and teens crave validation, and predators take advantage of this by:

- Complimenting the child excessively.
- Making them feel special or unique.
- Telling them that they are more mature than others their age.

3. **Sympathy and Manipulation**

Predators often play on a child's emotions by pretending to need help or sharing fake personal struggles. They may say things like:

- "I don't have anyone to talk to. You're the only one who understands me."
- "My parents don't care about me. I wish I had someone like you."
- "You're so mature for your age. I feel like I can trust you with anything."

4. Grooming Through Secret Conversations

Once they gain a child's trust, predators try to isolate them from others. They may:

- Encourage the child to keep their conversations secret from parents or friends.
- Move conversations to private messaging apps that are harder for parents to monitor.
- Discourage them from talking to other trusted adults about their online interactions.

5. Offering Gifts or Rewards

Predators may send virtual gifts, game items, or even money to win a child's trust. They may:

- Offer free in-game currency, premium memberships, or access to exclusive content.
- Give them real-world gifts like phones, clothes, or money in exchange for photos or videos.

6. Pressuring for Photos or Personal Information

Once trust is established, predators often escalate their demands. They might:

- Ask the child to send selfies, then slowly request more revealing photos.
- Trick them into sending personal details, such as their address or school name.
- Threaten to share private conversations if the child does not comply.

Understanding these tactics is the first step in protecting your child. The next section will help you recognize behavioral changes that could indicate your child is being targeted.

Warning Signs to Watch for in Your Child's Online Behavior

Children who are being groomed online may start showing unusual behaviors. If you notice any of the following signs, it may be time to have an open and supportive conversation with your child:

1. Increased Secrecy About Online Activity

- Quickly switching screens or closing tabs when someone enters the room.
- Refusing to share passwords or discuss who they are talking to online.
- Deleting messages or entire conversations from chat apps.

2. Sudden Mood Changes

- Becoming withdrawn, anxious, or secretive.
- Showing signs of distress after using the internet.
- Becoming irritable or defensive when asked about online interactions.

3. Unexplained Gifts or Money

- Receiving items like new gadgets, clothes, or money without a clear source.
- Hiding gifts or being vague about where they came from.

4. Talking to Strangers More Often

- Mentioning new online "friends" that they refuse to talk about in detail.
- Using unfamiliar apps or platforms you did not approve.

5. Changes in Sleep or School Performance

- Staying up late to use the internet when others are asleep.
- Declining performance in school or loss of interest in usual activities.
- If you notice these behaviors, take action immediately to ensure your child's safety.

Steps to Take If You Suspect Online Grooming

If you believe your child may be communicating with an online predator, follow these steps to protect them:

1. Stay Calm and Open a Conversation

- Approach your child with concern rather than anger.
- Ask open-ended questions: "Who do you talk to online? Have you made any new friends?"
- Listen without judgment so they feel safe sharing information.

2. Check Their Online Activity

- Review their chat history and social media accounts.
- Look for any hidden apps or secret messaging platforms.
- Check if they have multiple accounts on the same platform.

3. Strengthen Online Safety Measures

- Change passwords and enable parental controls.
- Restrict privacy settings on social media.
- Block suspicious contacts and report them.

4. Gather Evidence

- Take screenshots of concerning messages or images.
- Document dates, usernames, and any threats or requests made by the predator.
- Avoid deleting anything before reporting it to authorities.

Reporting Suspicious Activity

If you have confirmed or strongly suspect that an online predator is targeting your child, report it immediately. Here's how:

1. Report to the Platform

- Most social media, gaming, and messaging apps have a "Report" feature.
- Report the user for inappropriate behavior and block them.

2. Contact Law Enforcement

- File a report with your local police department.
- Contact national cybercrime units that specialize in online child exploitation.

3. Use Child Protection Organizations

- Many countries have child protection agencies that handle online safety concerns.

- Reach out to organizations that specialize in preventing child exploitation online.

4. Educate Your Child for Future Prevention

- Teach them about safe internet use and how to recognize red flags.
- Encourage open communication so they feel comfortable reporting any uncomfortable interactions.

Final Thoughts

Protecting your child from online predators requires vigilance, education, and proactive measures. By understanding how predators operate, recognizing the warning signs, and taking immediate action, you can safeguard your child's online experiences. Regular conversations about online safety and setting clear digital boundaries will help your child navigate the internet with confidence and awareness. Stay involved, stay informed, and most importantly, create an environment where your child feels safe discussing their online experiences with you.

Part 5: Advanced Strategies for Digital Parenting

Chapter 12: Raising Tech-Savvy and Responsible Digital Citizens

The internet is an incredible resource that allows children to learn, connect, and explore the world in ways that were unimaginable a few decades ago. However, with this power comes responsibility. As parents and educators, it is our duty to raise tech-savvy children who understand how to use digital tools wisely, safely, and ethically.

This chapter will guide you through essential aspects of digital citizenship, including teaching kids ethical online behavior, helping them navigate misinformation and fake news, and encouraging responsible technology use in schools. By the end of this section, you will have a clear strategy for preparing your child to thrive in the digital world while making smart, ethical choices online.

Teaching Kids Ethical Online Behavior

What is Ethical Online Behavior?

Ethical online behavior means using the internet and digital platforms in a way that is respectful, responsible, and mindful of others. It includes understanding the consequences of one's digital actions, treating others with kindness, and protecting one's own privacy and security. Just as children learn how to behave in the real world, they also need guidance on how to act in the digital space.

Why Ethical Online Behavior Matters

Teaching children to act responsibly online is crucial because:

- **Digital footprints are permanent.** Anything they post can be saved, shared, and accessed years later.
- **Cyberbullying and online harassment are real issues.** Children must learn that their words and actions online have real-world consequences.
- **Respecting privacy protects them and others.** Oversharing personal information can lead to security risks.
- **Plagiarism and copyright laws apply online.** Understanding intellectual property prevents unintentional wrongdoing.

Steps to Teach Ethical Online Behavior

- **Start with the Golden Rule** – Teach kids that if they wouldn't say something to someone's face, they shouldn't say it online. Words and actions have real impact.
- **Discuss Digital Footprints** – Show children how everything they post or share stays online. Help them think before they post.
- **Introduce Cyber Etiquette** – Teach them how to write polite messages, comment respectfully, and avoid engaging in online arguments.
- **Explain Cyberbullying** – Help them recognize when online behavior crosses the line into bullying and encourage them to stand against it.

- **Teach the Importance of Privacy** – Show them how to use privacy settings, avoid oversharing, and protect personal information.
- **Explain Copyright and Plagiarism** – Make them aware that copying content without permission is stealing. Encourage them to create original work.
- **Set Family Internet Rules** – Establish boundaries about what is appropriate to share, post, and say online.
- **Encourage Reporting and Seeking Help** – Teach them how to report inappropriate behavior and come to you when they feel uncomfortable about something online.

By setting clear expectations and modeling ethical behavior yourself, you help your child develop a strong moral compass for online interactions.

Helping Kids Navigate Misinformation and Fake News

Understanding Misinformation and Fake News

In today's digital world, information spreads quickly—both true and false. Misinformation refers to false or misleading information that is spread, regardless of intent. Fake news, on the other hand, is deliberately created to deceive people. Teaching children how to differentiate between real and false information is crucial to developing critical thinking skills.

Why This is Important

- **False information can mislead and manipulate.** It can shape opinions based on lies.
- **Fake news can be harmful.** Spreading misinformation can cause unnecessary panic or harm reputations.
- **Children are frequent targets.** Advertisers, scammers, and influencers may try to trick young users into believing false claims.
- **Learning critical thinking skills prepares them for life.** The ability to question and verify information is essential in the digital age.

Steps to Help Kids Identify Fake News

- **Teach Them to Question Sources** – Encourage children to ask, "Who wrote this? Where did this information come from?"
- **Look for Reliable Websites** – Show them how to identify trusted news sites and official sources.
- **Check the Date** – Old news can be misleading if it is shared as if it just happened.
- **Beware of Sensational Headlines** – Clickbait headlines often exaggerate facts to get attention.
- **Verify with Multiple Sources** – Encourage cross-checking news from different outlets before believing it.
- **Explain How Images and Videos Can Be Manipulated** – Teach them that photos and videos can be altered to mislead viewers.
- **Use Fact-Checking Websites** – Introduce them to sites like Snopes or FactCheck.org where they can verify news claims.

- **Encourage Open Discussions** – Make it a habit to discuss news with your child, helping them analyze and think critically about what they read.

By teaching children how to recognize and avoid fake news, you empower them to become informed and responsible digital citizens.

Encouraging Responsible Technology Use in Schools

The Role of Schools in Digital Citizenship

Schools play a crucial role in teaching children how to use technology responsibly. With the increasing reliance on digital tools for education, it's essential to establish guidelines that promote learning while preventing misuse.

Benefits of Responsible Technology Use in Schools

- **Enhances learning experiences.** Digital tools provide access to interactive learning resources.
- **Encourages collaboration.** Online platforms enable teamwork among students.
- **Prepares students for the digital workplace.** Familiarity with technology is essential for future careers.
- **Prevents distractions.** Clear guidelines help students stay focused on educational content rather than entertainment.

How Parents and Schools Can Promote Responsible Technology Use

- **Set Clear Guidelines for Digital Device Use** – Schools should establish policies on when and how students can use devices in class.
- **Monitor Online Activities in School Settings** – Teachers should oversee students' use of technology to ensure appropriate use.
- **Educate Students About Digital Citizenship** – Schools should include digital literacy as part of their curriculum.
- **Encourage the Use of Educational Apps** – Instead of banning devices, guide students toward using them for learning purposes.
- **Promote Breaks from Screen Time** – Schools should encourage outdoor activities and non-digital learning to balance screen use.
- **Train Teachers on Digital Safety** – Educators should be equipped with knowledge on how to guide students in responsible tech use.
- **Encourage Parental Involvement** – Parents should stay informed about their child's digital activities in school and reinforce the rules at home.

By working together, schools and parents can create a safe and constructive digital learning environment.

Conclusion

Raising tech-savvy and responsible digital citizens requires patience, education, and consistent reinforcement of ethical online behavior. By teaching kids to use technology responsibly, think critically about online information, and follow digital rules in school, we prepare them to navigate the online world with confidence and integrity.

Start the conversation today, set clear guidelines, and empower your child to make smart choices in their digital interactions. The internet is a powerful tool—let's ensure our children use it wisely and safely.

Chapter 13: Preparing for the Future of Technology

Technology is evolving at an astonishing pace, and as parents, it is crucial to stay informed about emerging trends that will shape our children's digital world. The internet today is vastly different from what it was a decade ago, and in the coming years, advancements in artificial intelligence (AI), virtual reality (VR), and the metaverse will redefine how kids interact with the digital landscape.

Understanding these changes can help parents make informed decisions, set the right boundaries, and equip their children with the skills they need to navigate the future of technology safely and responsibly. In this chapter, we will explore key technological trends, their impact on children's online experiences, and how parents can prepare their kids for a future dominated by digital innovations.

The Rise of AI, Virtual Reality, and the Metaverse

Technology is no longer just about websites and social media. The digital world is becoming more immersive, intelligent, and interactive. Three of the most significant advancements shaping the future include artificial intelligence, virtual reality, and the metaverse.

Artificial Intelligence (AI)

AI is already a part of daily life, from voice assistants like Alexa and Siri to recommendation algorithms on YouTube and Netflix. However, AI is becoming more sophisticated, with capabilities such as:

- **Personalized learning** – AI-driven educational tools can customize lessons to match a child's learning style and pace.
- **Chatbots and virtual tutors** – AI-powered tutors can assist students with homework and provide explanations tailored to their needs.
- **Content generation** – AI tools can create stories, images, and videos, allowing children to engage in creative activities like never before.
- **Deepfake and misinformation risks** – AI can generate realistic but false content, making it harder to distinguish between real and fake information.

Virtual Reality (VR)

Virtual reality takes digital experiences to the next level by allowing users to immerse themselves in a 3D environment. VR headsets like the Oculus Quest and PlayStation VR are growing in popularity, and the applications for children include:

- **Educational field trips** – Kids can explore historical sites, outer space, or the deep ocean from their living rooms.
- **Skill development** – VR simulations can teach coding, engineering, art, and other valuable skills in an interactive way.

- **Gaming and social interaction** – VR gaming is becoming more realistic and engaging, but it also introduces risks such as addiction and cyberbullying in virtual worlds.

The Metaverse

The metaverse is an evolving concept that refers to a collective virtual space where people can interact using digital avatars. Platforms like Roblox, Fortnite, and Meta's Horizon Worlds are early examples of this technology. In the metaverse, children can:

- **Socialize and create** – They can build virtual worlds, design characters, and interact with others in a shared digital space.
- **Work and learn** – Schools and businesses are exploring the use of the metaverse for virtual classrooms and remote workspaces.
- **Face new safety concerns** – The metaverse raises concerns about privacy, online predators, and excessive screen time.

How Emerging Tech Will Change Kids' Online Experience

The digital world that today's children grow up with will be vastly different from the one their parents experienced. Here's how emerging technology will reshape kids' online interactions:

1. Increased Personalization

AI-driven algorithms will continue to shape what children see online, from recommended videos to suggested friends. While this can enhance learning and entertainment, it also means children might get trapped in echo chambers where they only see one type of content.

2. More Immersive Social Interactions

With the rise of VR and the metaverse, children's online interactions will become more immersive. Instead of simply texting or video chatting, they may enter virtual spaces and engage in life-like conversations with friends, teachers, and even strangers.

3. Enhanced Learning Opportunities

AI and VR will revolutionize education, making learning more engaging and interactive. Imagine a child studying ancient Egypt by walking through a realistic VR simulation of the pyramids or learning physics by manipulating virtual objects.

4. New Digital Dangers

As technology advances, so do online risks. Deepfake technology can create highly convincing fake videos, making it harder to discern real from fake information. The metaverse may expose children to new forms of cyberbullying and online exploitation.

Preparing Kids for Future Digital Trends

Technology will continue to evolve, but parents can take proactive steps to ensure their children are prepared for the future. Here's how:

1. Teach Critical Thinking and Media Literacy

Children must learn how to analyze information critically. Teach them to:

- Question the reliability of online sources.
- Recognize deepfakes and AI-generated misinformation.
- Understand how algorithms influence what they see online.

2. Set Boundaries for New Technologies

Just as screen time limits are essential today, parents must establish rules for future technologies:

- Define appropriate usage times for VR and metaverse activities.
- Ensure kids take regular breaks from immersive digital experiences.
- Discuss digital well-being and maintaining a balance between online and offline activities.

3. Emphasize Online Safety in Virtual Worlds

As virtual reality and the metaverse become more integrated into daily life, safety precautions should be a priority:

- Encourage kids to use avatars and usernames that don't reveal personal information.
- Teach them to recognize suspicious behavior and report inappropriate activities.
- Monitor their interactions in virtual spaces to ensure they engage with safe and appropriate content.

4. Encourage Hands-on Tech Learning

Understanding how technology works will help children navigate it safely and responsibly. Consider introducing them to:

- Coding platforms like Scratch or Tynker to build basic programming skills.
- Robotics kits that teach engineering and problem-solving.
- AI-powered tools that allow kids to experiment with machine learning in a safe environment.

5. Stay Informed and Evolve with Technology

Technology is always changing, and staying informed is crucial. Parents should:

- Keep up with the latest advancements in AI, VR, and online safety.
- Join parenting forums or follow digital literacy experts to stay updated.
- Engage in discussions with their children about new technologies and their potential impact.

Conclusion

The future of technology is filled with exciting opportunities and new challenges. AI, virtual reality, and the metaverse will redefine how children interact with the digital world, offering innovative ways to learn, socialize, and create. However, with these advancements come new risks, making it essential for parents to educate themselves and guide their children through this evolving landscape.

By fostering critical thinking, setting clear boundaries, and encouraging hands-on learning, parents can equip their children with the skills and awareness needed to thrive in the digital age. The key to successful digital parenting is not to fear new technology but to embrace it with informed and proactive strategies that prioritize safety, education, and balance.

Conclusion

As we reach the conclusion of this book, it is important to reflect on the essential role that parents play in shaping their children's digital behavior. The online world is vast, exciting, and full of opportunities, but it also comes with risks that can be overwhelming for both children and parents. By taking an active role in guiding and protecting your child's online journey, you create a safer, healthier, and more balanced digital environment for them to grow and thrive.

The Role of Parents in Shaping Digital Behavior

Children are naturally curious and eager to explore the digital world, and their habits are often influenced by what they see at home. As a parent, you are the first and most important role model in their digital journey. Your approach to technology, screen time, and online interactions will significantly impact how your child views and engages with the internet.

Setting a Positive Example

Your children will learn from your digital habits, so it's important to demonstrate healthy online behavior. If they see you prioritizing real-world interactions, managing screen time wisely, and handling online challenges with care, they are more likely to adopt those behaviors themselves.

- Avoid excessive screen time in front of your child.
- Show responsible social media use, including respectful conversations and privacy awareness.
- Practice balanced tech use, such as putting away devices during family meals or outdoor activities.

Being Actively Involved

Being a passive observer of your child's digital habits is not enough. Instead, you should take an active role in understanding and monitoring their online activities. This does not mean invading their privacy, but rather being present, engaged, and aware.

- Have regular conversations about what they do online.
- Explore apps, games, and websites together to understand their appeal.
- Encourage them to come to you if they encounter anything uncomfortable online.

Teaching Digital Responsibility

Digital responsibility is just as important as offline manners and ethics. Help your child understand that their online actions have consequences, just as they do in real life.

- Educate them about online etiquette, including being kind and respectful.
- Discuss the importance of privacy and the risks of oversharing.

- Encourage critical thinking when consuming online information, helping them identify fake news and scams.

Final Digital Parenting Checklist

To help you apply everything you have learned in this book, here is a final checklist to guide your approach to digital parenting. This checklist summarizes the key actions you should take to create a safe and healthy digital environment for your child.

Basic Online Safety Measures

✅ Set up parental controls on devices and apps.
✅ Enable privacy settings on social media accounts.
✅ Educate your child about safe browsing and online threats.
✅ Ensure they use strong passwords and two-factor authentication.

Healthy Digital Habits

✅ Establish screen time limits and enforce them consistently.
✅ Create tech-free zones, such as during meals and before bedtime.
✅ Encourage a balance between online and offline activities.
✅ Lead by example with responsible technology use.

Monitoring & Supervision

✅ Regularly check the apps, websites, and games your child is using.
✅ Discuss their online experiences openly and regularly.
✅ Teach them how to report and block inappropriate content or

users.

✓ Monitor for signs of cyberbullying or online stress.

Encouraging Digital Responsibility

✓ Teach your child about ethical online behavior.

✓ Discuss the risks of oversharing personal information.

✓ Help them recognize fake news and misinformation.

✓ Encourage kindness, empathy, and respect in online interactions.

By following this checklist, you can create a structured approach to digital parenting that is proactive, supportive, and effective.

Encouraging Open Communication About Online Safety

One of the most important aspects of digital parenting is maintaining open and honest communication with your child. They should feel comfortable coming to you with any concerns, questions, or experiences they encounter online. A strong foundation of trust ensures that your child will turn to you for guidance rather than hiding their digital activities.

Creating a Judgment-Free Environment

Children may make mistakes online, such as clicking on a suspicious link or engaging in conversations with strangers. If they fear being punished or judged, they may hide these experiences from you, putting them at greater risk. Instead of reacting with anger, use these moments as learning opportunities.

- Listen without immediate judgment or punishment.
- Ask them what happened and how they felt about it.
- Offer guidance on what they should do differently next time.

Encouraging Regular Conversations

Make internet safety an ongoing conversation rather than a one-time discussion. The digital landscape is constantly evolving, and new risks emerge all the time.

- Ask about their favorite websites, games, and online friends.
- Discuss new trends and potential risks they might face.
- Share your own experiences with online safety to make the conversation relatable.

Teaching Them to Speak Up

Children should know that they can always come to you if something makes them uncomfortable online. Encourage them to:

- Report cyberbullying immediately.
- Tell you if they encounter inappropriate content.
- Ask for help before making online purchases or signing up for new accounts.

Building Digital Confidence

Rather than scaring your child about online dangers, empower them with knowledge and confidence to navigate the digital world safely. When children feel informed and capable, they are more likely to make smart choices online.

Final Thoughts

Digital parenting is an ongoing journey that evolves as technology advances and your child grows. While challenges may arise, the key is to stay engaged, informed, and proactive. By fostering open communication, setting clear boundaries, and guiding your child toward responsible digital behavior, you can create a safer and healthier online environment for them.

Your role as a parent is not to completely shield your child from the digital world but to equip them with the skills, knowledge, and confidence they need to navigate it safely and responsibly. By implementing the strategies outlined in this book, you are taking a significant step toward ensuring your child's digital well-being.

Remember, you are not alone in this journey. Many parents face the same struggles and concerns, and by staying connected with parenting communities and staying updated on digital trends, you can continue to adapt and protect your child effectively.

Thank you for taking the time to learn about digital parenting. Your efforts will have a lasting impact on your child's safety, confidence, and ability to thrive in the digital world.

Additional Resources

In today's digital world, parents need reliable tools and trusted platforms to help guide their children's online experiences. This section provides two essential resources:

- A **Parental Control Apps Comparison Chart**, which helps parents choose the best app for their needs.
- A **List of Safe Websites & Apps for Kids**, offering kid-friendly digital spaces where children can explore, learn, and play safely.

Parental Control Apps Comparison Chart

One of the most effective ways to supervise and guide your child's online activities is by using parental control apps. These apps provide essential features such as content filtering, screen time management, location tracking, and activity monitoring. However, with so many options available, it can be overwhelming to determine which one is the best fit for your family.

To simplify this decision, the following comparison chart breaks down the key features of popular parental control apps, allowing you to compare their strengths and limitations at a glance.

What to Look for in a Parental Control App

Before diving into the chart, let's briefly discuss the most important features parents should consider when selecting a parental control app:

- **Content Filtering:** Blocks access to inappropriate websites, apps, and content based on age and category.
- **Screen Time Management:** Allows parents to set daily limits on device usage and schedule screen-free times.
- **App Blocking & Control:** Lets parents prevent access to specific apps or set restrictions on their use.
- **Location Tracking & Geo-Fencing:** Helps monitor a child's real-time location and sends alerts if they enter restricted areas.
- **Social Media Monitoring:** Tracks activity on platforms like Instagram, TikTok, and Snapchat, detecting potential risks.
- **Call & Text Monitoring:** Lets parents review calls and messages to detect potential dangers (availability varies by app and device).
- **Remote Control & Alerts:** Allows parents to pause the internet, lock devices remotely, and receive alerts about concerning activity.
- **Ease of Use & Compatibility:** The app should be easy to set up and compatible with the devices your child uses (iOS, Android, Windows, Mac, etc.).

Parental Control Apps: Feature Comparison

Feature	Qustodio	Bark	Net Nanny	Norton Family	Google Family Link	Apple Screen Time
Content Filtering	✅	✅	✅	✅	✅	✅
Screen Time Management	✅	✅	✅	✅	✅	✅
App Blocking & Control	✅	❌	✅	✅	✅	✅
Social Media Monitoring	✅	✅	❌	❌	❌	❌
Location Tracking	✅	✅	✅	✅	✅	❌
Call & Text Monitoring	✅ (Android Only)	✅ (Android Only)	❌	❌	❌	❌
Remote Control & Alerts	✅	✅	✅	✅	❌	✅
Best For	Full control	Social media monitoring	Web filtering	Family-wide control	Basic monitoring	Apple users

Note: Some features may require a premium subscription or work differently on iOS vs. Android devices.

Choosing the Right App for Your Family

If you need **comprehensive control**, **Qustodio** or **Net Nanny** are great options. If your main concern is **social media monitoring**, **Bark** is designed specifically for that. **Google Family Link** is free and works well for younger kids, while **Apple Screen Time** is a good built-in option for iOS users. **Norton Family** is best for families who want a balance between web filtering and time management.

No single app is perfect, so consider your child's age, online habits, and the level of monitoring you need before making a decision.

List of Safe Websites & Apps for Kids

The internet can be an incredible place for learning, creativity, and entertainment—if children have access to safe, kid-friendly platforms. This list includes websites and apps that offer engaging, age-appropriate content while maintaining strong safety measures.

Educational Websites & Apps

- **PBS Kids (www.pbskids.org)** – Interactive games, videos, and educational content featuring popular PBS characters.
- **National Geographic Kids (kids.nationalgeographic.com)** – Fun facts, games, and videos about science, nature, and animals.
- **Khan Academy Kids (App)** – Free educational games and lessons designed for young learners.
- **Duolingo Kids (App)** – A fun way for kids to learn new languages through interactive lessons.

Creative & Interactive Platforms

- **Scratch (scratch.mit.edu)** – A safe coding platform where kids can create animations and games.
- **Tynker (www.tynker.com)** – Coding lessons and games that teach kids the basics of programming.
- **LEGO Life (App)** – A creative space where kids can share LEGO builds and interact with other young LEGO fans in a safe environment.
- **Crayola Create & Play (App)** – Art games, coloring pages, and creative challenges for kids.

Safe Video Streaming & Storytelling Apps

- **YouTube Kids (App & website)** – A child-friendly version of YouTube with curated, age-appropriate videos.
- **Epic! (www.getepic.com)** – A digital library with thousands of kid-friendly books and audiobooks.
- **Storytime Online (www.storylineonline.net)** – Celebrities read children's books aloud, making reading fun and engaging.
- **Audiobooks.com (Kids Section)** – A collection of audiobooks designed for young listeners.

Kid-Friendly Games & Virtual Worlds

- **Minecraft (Education Edition)** – A creative sandbox game with educational features for kids.
- **Roblox (Parental Controls Needed)** – A popular platform where kids can play games created by other users. Parents should use safety settings.
- **Animal Jam (www.animaljam.com)** – A safe online game that teaches kids about animals and nature.
- **ABCmouse (www.abcmouse.com)** – Educational games and activities for early learners.

Safe Communication Apps for Kids

- **Messenger Kids (App)** – A safer version of Facebook Messenger designed for kids, allowing parents to monitor contacts.
- **Google Family Link (App Feature)** – Allows controlled communication while keeping kids safe.

- **Kinzoo (App)** – A safe messaging app designed for young kids, free from ads and tracking.

Final Thoughts

Digital parenting isn't just about blocking bad content—it's about guiding children toward safe, enriching, and age-appropriate online experiences. By combining parental control tools with a selection of trusted, kid-friendly platforms, parents can empower their children to explore the digital world safely.

www.ingramcontent.com/pod-product-compliance
Lightning Source LLC
LaVergne TN
LVHW051736050326
832903LV00023B/942